D1503892

SCIENCE AND TECHNOLOGY START-UP STARS

SPACE Entrepreneurs

James Bow

CRABTREE
PUBLISHING COMPANY
WWW.CRABTREEBOOKS.COM

CRABTREE
PUBLISHING COMPANY
WWW.CRABTREEBOOKS.COM

Author: James Bow

Editors: Sarah Eason, Nancy Dickmann, Wendy Scavuzzo, and Petrice Custance

Proofreader and indexer: Wendy Scavuzzo

Editorial director: Kathy Middleton

Design: Clare Webber

Cover design and additional artwork: Clare Webber

Photo research: Rachel Blount

Production coordinator and Prepress technician: Tammy McGarr

Print coordinator: Katherine Berti

Consultant: David Hawksett

Produced for Crabtree Publishing Company by Calcium Creative

Photo Credits:

t=Top, tr=Top Right, tl=Top Left

Inside: Accion Systems: pp. 12, 13; Alamy/ZUMA Press, Inc.: p. 16; Mars World Enterprises, Inc. © 2017 All rights reserved: pp. 3, 14, 15b; NASA: pp. 10, 22, 23b, 26, 27b; NASA Goddard Space Flight Center: p. 21b; NASA/JPL-Caltech: p. 20; Sally Ride EarthKAM: p. 10; Shutterstock: Cowardlion: p. 29t; Georgios Kollidas: p. 5t; SAHACHATZ: p. 19t; U.S. Air Force: Christopher DeWitt: p. 29b; Ken LaRock: p. 27t; Wikimedia Commons: DLR (CC-BY 3.0): p. 15t; FranksValli: p. 21t; Steve Jurvetson: pp. 9t, 24; Don Ramey Logan: p. 7b; NASA: pp. 11b, 17, 18, 23t, 25; NASA; restored by Adam Cuerden: p. 7tr; NASA/Expedition 31: p. 5b; NASA/Human Systems Engineering and Development Division: p. 8; NASA Langley Research Center: p. 7tl; Daphne Weld Nichols: p. 6; Recentcontributor2000: p. 11t; SpaceX Photos: pp. 4, 9b, 28.

Cover: Shutterstock: Sergey Nivens.

Library and Archives Canada Cataloguing in Publication

Bow, James, 1972-, author
    Space entrepreneurs / James Bow.

(Science and technology start-up stars)
Includes index.
Issued in print and electronic formats.
ISBN 978-0-7787-4423-8 (hardcover).--
ISBN 978-0-7787-4436-8 (softcover).--
ISBN 978-1-4271-2027-4 (HTML)

    1. Astronautics--Technological innovations--Juvenile literature.
2. Outer space--Exploration--Technological innovations--Juvenile
literature. 3. Entrepreneurship--Juvenile literature. I. Title.

TL793.B695 2018   j629.4   C2017-907707-4
                              C2017-907708-2

Library of Congress Cataloging-in-Publication Data

CIP available at the Library of Congress

Crabtree Publishing Company

www.crabtreebooks.com   1-800-387-7650

Printed in the U.S.A./022018/CG20171220

Copyright © **2018 CRABTREE PUBLISHING COMPANY**. All rights reserved. No part of this publication may be reproduced, stored in a retrieval system or be transmitted in any form or by any means, electronic, mechanical, photocopying, recording, or otherwise, without the prior written permission of Crabtree Publishing Company. In Canada: We acknowledge the financial support of the Government of Canada through the Canada Book Fund for our publishing activities.

Published in Canada
Crabtree Publishing
616 Welland Ave.
St. Catharines, Ontario
L2M 5V6

Published in the United States
Crabtree Publishing
PMB 59051
350 Fifth Avenue, 59th Floor
New York, New York 10118

Published in the United Kingdom
Crabtree Publishing
Maritime House
Basin Road North, Hove
BN41 1WR

Published in Australia
Crabtree Publishing
3 Charles Street
Coburg North
VIC, 3058

CONTENTS

YOU CAN BE AN ENTREPRENEUR!

On April 8, 2016, Elon Musk's SpaceX rocket Falcon 9 launched. Its **first stage booster rocket** came off as planned, and fell toward the ocean. The rocket successfully landed on a **drone ship**. Most other rockets fall back to Earth and are destroyed. Musk's Falcon 9 was a solution to these one-time-use rockets. By reusing its booster rockets, the Falcon 9 saves both energy and waste. It is an example of how brilliant **entrepreneurs** are using their skills in space science.

ENTREPRENEURS AND START-UPS

An entrepreneur is someone who plans, starts, and runs a business that provides **goods** or **services**. Entrepreneurs are people who take risks to develop new products and start new businesses. They sometimes have an original or **innovative** idea, then turn that idea into a business that supplies those goods or services. Start-ups are brand-new businesses created by entrepreneurs.

ENTREPRENEURS CHANGING THE WORLD

The world is changing at a fast pace. New technologies are being introduced that change the way we live and work. We face many challenges, including **overpopulation**, **global warming**, and the depletion of natural resources. However, we can tackle these challenges using science and technology if we think creatively, solve problems, and work together. By exploring the possibilities that space offers, many innovative entrepreneurs are doing just that.

To land the booster rocket so that it could be reused, SpaceX had to calculate exactly where it would fall.

Early Thinkers

Scientists and engineers throughout history have helped us get into space. Isaac Newton (1642–1726) studied science and mathematics from a young age. When he was in his early 20s, he helped invent calculus. Calculus is a special type of math that can help explain how planets move. It was Newton who first figured out that if a cannonball was fired fast enough, it would fall beyond the curve of Earth. The cannonball would keep falling, eventually circling the planet.

The work of Isaac Newton made it possible for later scientists and entrepreneurs to investigate space.

ENTREPRENEURS OF THE FUTURE

Elon Musk is just one of many young entrepreneurs who are joining the race to space. Space-tech start-up companies are launching **satellites**. They are bringing tourists to space. Some are even planning to mine **asteroids**. Perhaps you will one day follow in their footsteps, launching your own start-up into a whole new world!

SpaceX hopes that its Dragon **capsule** will one day take astronauts to the **International Space Station (ISS)**.

INTO SPACE

Space exploration relies on science, technology, engineering, and math. Scientists, engineers, and researchers must understand how rockets work. They need to know how to engineer the rocket technology to leave Earth. They need mathematics to predict where the rockets will go, and how they will act once in space. Space science involves the skills of many researchers. Until recently, only governments had the workforce and money needed to get people and things into space.

DOING THE NUMBERS

In the 1950s, the United States and the **Soviet Union** were involved in a space race. Each country's government worked hard to put the first satellite in space. That was followed by the first animal and the first person. Before the age of computers, NASA scientists had to calculate rocket flight paths using pencils, paper, and **slide rules**. A lot of math had to be done by hand. Many men and women worked at NASA to check the math.

These mathematicians included Mary Jackson and Katherine Johnson, two young African-American women. Their brilliant math skills helped astronaut John Glenn to become the first American to **orbit** Earth. Their work has been recognized in the book and movie *Hidden Figures*. At the time, computer scientists such as Margaret Hamilton had to write code by hand. She programmed the computers that powered the Apollo rockets. The Soviet Union put the first satellite and first person into space. But thanks to the work of NASA's scientists and mathematicians, the United States won the race to get the first person on the Moon.

Margaret Hamilton helped write the navigation code for the Apollo mission. When it was printed out and stacked up, the code was as tall as she was.

Mary Jackson taught math and worked as a secretary before joining NASA.

Katherine Johnson started high school at the age of 10.

The Rocketeers

The Ansari XPRIZE was created in May 1996 by the XPRIZE Foundation. Its founders hoped that the competition would encourage people to come up with safe and affordable ways to travel to space. The prize would be awarded to any private company that developed a reusable spacecraft. It had to be capable of carrying three people to at least 62 miles (100 km) above Earth. And the spacecraft had to do so twice in two weeks!

The prize was won eight years later, in 2004, by the American company Mojave **Aerospace** Ventures. It developed the spacecraft SpaceShipOne, designed by space science whiz Burt Rutan. The first flight was launched on September 29, 2004, flown by Mike Melvill. Less than one week later, Brian Binnie flew the winning flight to space.

Burt Rutan began designing model aircraft when he was eight years old.

ROCKET
START-UP STAR:
ELON MUSK

Elon Musk is a well-known high-tech entrepreneur. He had helped found PayPal, which was sold to eBay for $1.5 billion. He used his share of the sale to set up Tesla, Inc. He has already had a major impact on the world.

A MARTIAN OASIS

Musk has always been interested in space. In 2001, he proposed making an **oasis** on Mars. His idea was to land a small greenhouse on the planet, with seeds in a special **fertilizer** to help them grow in Martian soil. The plants could help supply a future Mars **colony**. Musk hoped to build public interest in exploring space, and to increase NASA's **budget**.

Musk realized that traveling to Mars using current rockets would be too slow and expensive. He looked for ways to encourage private companies to research space travel to make it cheaper and easier. In 2002, he helped set up the private company SpaceX. SpaceX works to make rockets less expensive and more reliable. He took some big risks to do this. Musk invested in expensive equipment to make SpaceX's rockets before knowing whether they could get into space. However, he knew that if he could make his rockets work, he could get a lot of business. Up to then, the job of launching satellites and supplying space stations was in the hands of a few government space agencies. Private companies did not play a big role in space business.

Greenhouses on Mars would allow colonists to grow their own food.

FALCON

A *Star Wars* fan, Musk named SpaceX's experimental rocket Falcon, after the movie's *Millennium Falcon* spaceship. However, the first few Falcon launches ended in failure, and the company almost went **bankrupt** in 2008. But Musk persisted, and SpaceX launched the first privately funded, liquid–fueled rocket to reach orbit on September 28, 2008. It became the first private space company to dock, or anchor, with the International Space Station in 2012. The company sent its first satellite into **geosynchronous orbit** on December 3, 2015. It was also the first private company to send a probe outside Earth's orbit on February 11, 2015.

SpaceX is now focused on recovering and reusing its rockets to save money and energy. On April 8, 2016, SpaceX successfully guided a booster rocket onto a drone ship on the ocean. Musk hopes that SpaceX's work will make space travel more common.

Elon Musk has led the way in space entrepreneurship.

SpaceX rockets have already delivered scientific gear and crew supplies to the International Space Station.

AROUND THE WORLD

Satellites look down on Earth with cameras and other instruments to watch, map, and measure the world. They provide us with astonishing images of our planet that can only be seen from space. They can receive signals from one part of the world and send them to the other side of the planet.

SPACE ROBOTS

Sputnik was the first satellite launched into space. Created by the Soviet Union, it was a sphere 22.8 inches (58 cm) in diameter with four radio antennae. It circled Earth starting on October 4, 1957. It only lasted 21 days, sending beeps back to mission control, but it proved that it was possible to send satellites into orbit. As computers got smaller and more complex, they were put into later satellites to help them do more things. For example, satellites with **radar** or lasers measure clouds and surface and air temperatures. This information helps **meteorologists** and climate scientists.

Satellites in orbit allow us to see our planet from a different perspective, such as this bird's-eye view of the Grand Canyon.

PUTTING BUSINESS INTO ORBIT

The first private satellite was built by AT&T and Bell Telephone Laboratories—two huge companies that could spend millions on research and development. But the satellite still had to be launched into orbit by NASA. Only governments had the **resources** to put things into space. On July 10, 1962, Telstar 1 was launched. It was a communications satellite that could receive signals from one part of Earth and beam them instantly to receivers on the other side of the planet. Satellites such as Telstar 1 are why we can phone distant countries and get news instantly from around the world.

At first, entrepreneurs bought signal space from the large companies that owned satellites. For example, Lon Levin founded the American Mobile Satellite Corporation in 1988 to create a satellite radio network. His company went on to launch its own satellites around 2001. One problem with making your own satellite is that you have to pay someone to launch it, and rocket space is limited. However, another innovative company, Rocket Lab (founded in 2006 by Peter Beck), is designing smaller, cheaper rockets. These rockets could lower the cost of getting small satellites into orbit.

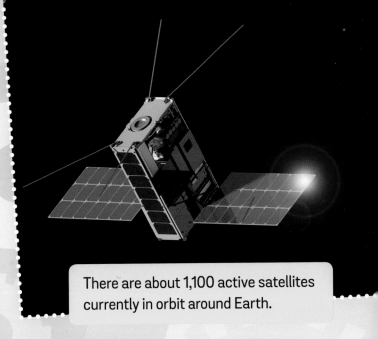

There are about 1,100 active satellites currently in orbit around Earth.

Satellite Trash Collector

When satellites stop working, they become space trash. More than 21,000 pieces of space litter, 4 inches (10 cm) or larger, float around Earth. Japanese entrepreneur Mitsunobu Okada created the start-up Astroscale. He wants to clean up space litter. He designed ELSA 1, a robot spaceship that can move around to catch the trash with panels coated in glue. Once full, ELSA would fall out of orbit, burning itself and the trash up when it enters Earth's atmosphere. Satellite companies would pay Astroscale to clean up an area of space. They want to make sure nothing was around to damage their equipment.

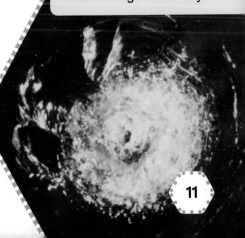

Even tiny objects can damage a spacecraft. This space shuttle window was damaged this way.

SATELLITE START-UP STARS:
NATALYA BAILEY AND LOUIS PERNA

Natalya (Brikner) Bailey and Louis Perna were Ph.D. classmates at the Massachusetts Institute of Technology (MIT). In 2014, they discovered a cheap and safe way to move satellites in space.

Bailey is interested in encouraging kids, especially girls, to study and get involved in science and technology. By acting as a mentor and positive role model, she hopes that more women will become entrepreneurs.

FALLING TO EARTH

Objects sent into space need rockets to move around. The energy released by burning fuel and pushing it out a nozzle produces a thrust in the opposite direction. However, rocket fuel is dangerous and heavy. Because of this, most small satellites are sent to space without rockets. This means they cannot maneuver when they reach orbit. With no way to steer, small satellites usually fall back to Earth within months.

ION POWER

Bailey and Perna designed an **ion** engine as an alternative to a traditional rocket. Instead of burning rocket fuel, their ion engine uses a process called electrospray to shoot out small charged particles called ions. The thrusters, or engines, designed by Bailey and Perna are very small—about the size of a postage stamp. But they can do a lot of work. Since satellites are weightless in space, the tiny thrusters can maneuver them in orbit. The ion thrusters also last a long time. This means that expensive satellites can do more work in the time they remain in orbit. The thrusters also mean that satellites can be kept small, because they do not require large engines. Sending smaller satellites into orbit uses less energy—which saves even more money.

In this image, we can see that Bailey and Perna's tiny thrusters are smaller than a quarter! They use liquid salt as fuel to make ions.

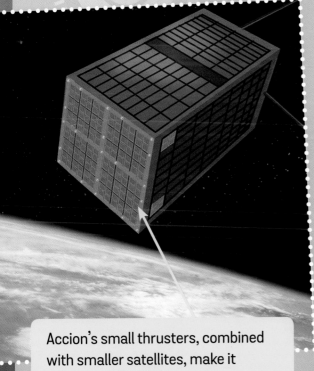

Accion's small thrusters, combined with smaller satellites, make it cheaper and easier to send important scientific equipment into space.

IMPORTANT CUSTOMERS

Bailey and Perna set up Accion Systems, a space tech company based on their idea. Accion is named after the Accio spell in the Harry Potter book series, which is used to summon things. Accion Systems raised millions of dollars from **investors**. They also scored a number of contracts from agencies looking to build smaller, more affordable satellites, including the U.S. military. Now the **CEO** of Accion, Bailey is working to help make satellites smaller and more affordable, and to create more powerful propulsion systems to push space exploration forward. She also acts as a mentor to those at younger start-up companies. She hopes to encourage new entrepreneurs to reach their goals.

SPACE TOURISM

If you could travel to space, or visit Mars, would you? People around the world say they would, and many entrepreneurs are looking at ways to help people do just that.

As of 2017, only 12 people have stood on the Moon. Only 536 have visited space. We need expensive equipment to launch people into space, and to keep them alive while they are there. Space travel is expensive, but the technology is improving and getting cheaper. Entrepreneurs hope more tourists may visit space soon.

Theme parks such as Mars World could give people a taste of what space is like—without leaving Earth!

ADVENTURES IN SPACE

American company Space Adventures was founded in 1998. Its first customer was the multimillionaire Dennis Tito. For $20 million, Space Adventures flew Tito aboard a Russian rocket to the ISS. As of 2017, Space Adventures is the only company that has taken tourists into space. Other companies have plans to, though. Richard Branson's Virgin Galactic, Jeff Bezos's Blue Origin, and Jeff Greason's XCOR Aerospace all have plans for vehicles that can take off from Earth. They will take passengers into space and back. As research continues, the technology should become affordable enough for more entrepreneurs to take on space tourism.

Zero-G planes can take off from any regular airport.

EXPERIENCE WEIGHTLESSNESS

For those who don't have the money or strength to handle a trip into space, they can still experience weightlessness, thanks to Zero G. The company was founded in 2004 by entrepreneur Peter Diamandis, along with NASA engineer Ray Cronise and astronaut Byron Lichtenberg. It uses large passenger airplanes with all of the seats removed. The plane flies in long **parabolas**, rising 9,000 feet (2,743 m) very quickly, then flying down at a 30-degree angle. The passengers inside experience weightlessness. They can float and swim in the middle of the plane, until the plane reaches the bottom of its dive and turns to fly up. Zero G flights are not just for tourists. NASA buys a ticket when it needs to test equipment in **microgravity**.

INSPIRING STORIES

Mars World

Maybe we don't need to leave Earth to explore other planets. John Spencer is a designer of space projects for NASA and space and future-themed entertainment projects. He thinks we can bring other planets to Earth. In Las Vegas, along with Lewis Stanton and Lisa Leight, Spencer is developing a version of a future city on Mars called Mars World. Visitors will be immersed in the first **extra-terrestrial** urban **environment**. They can interact with humans born on Mars and explore its futuristic culture!

Mars World visitors will be able to trek across a crater.

15

START-UP STAR:
ERIC ANDERSON

Eric Anderson was born in 1974 and studied aerospace engineering and computer science at the University of Virginia. Since childhood, he wanted to be an astronaut. At university, he interned with Peter Diamandis, the chair, or leader, of the XPRIZE Foundation. Anderson helped organize the Ansari XPRIZE competition, and took part in the NASA Academy in 1995. There, his thoughts turned toward space tourism and launching a start-up company.

TO THE GREAT BEYOND

With the help of Diamandis, Anderson founded Space Adventures in 1998, when he was just 23. The first flights for the company were onboard Russian MiG-25 fighter jets, which could fly to the edge of space. He made connections with the Russian Space Agency, and convinced them to sell space on their Soyuz capsules. They offered tourists a trip to the International Space Station. Convincing government space agencies to give up seats to private citizens took time, but Anderson reached an agreement with the Russian Space Agency in 1999. The first space tourist to fly to the International Space Station was American engineer and money manager Dennis Tito. He paid $20 million for the trip. Space

Adventures offers a number of different packages, from visits to the International Space Station to flying on a rocket that circles the Moon. No one has raised enough money to buy a ticket for the Moon trip, yet.

Entrepreneurs like Eric Anderson are paving the way for space tourism through their pioneering work.

SPACE ADVOCATE

Anderson has encouraged others to work toward moving people out into space. In 2010, he became chair of the Commercial Spaceflight Federation. It encourages aerospace businesses to work together to develop a spaceflight industry similar to the airline industry. Anderson has also founded Planetary Resources, Inc., a company that develops technology to explore asteroids and mine them for **minerals** and metals.

OTHER INTERESTS

In addition to looking to space, Anderson hopes to solve some problems here on Earth. In 2007, he helped found Planetary Power, Inc., a company that develops renewable energy technology that people can afford. He is also president of International Software, a company that helps other software companies design programs that people can understand, even if they are not familiar with computers.

Dennis Tito (far left) worked with the crew of the International Space Station.

SPACE DATA

Space provides us with a lot of data. Our militaries still use satellites to look down on the movements of armies or terrorist groups. Satellites help meteorologists predict the weather. They also tell drivers where they are and the best routes to take to their destination. Robot probes have been sent to other planets to send back photographs that help us learn more about these planets.

USING THE DATA

Sending and receiving data from space is a big challenge. NASA has worked with a number of entrepreneurs to improve satellite and space probe radio communications. This is to ensure that researchers on Earth can talk to space vehicles billions of miles away. It can take scientists months to process and **interpret** the data collected by space vehicles.

However, NASA puts its photos and a lot of its data in the public domain, which means that everyone can access it. The data from satellites can be used to improve the lives of people around the world. One example is the **global positioning system (GPS)**.

Photos from space can show human impact on Earth, such as light pollution caused by city lights.

GOING PUBLIC

GPS uses a network of satellites and **triangulation** to help people figure out where they are in the world with great accuracy. At first, GPS data was only available to the U.S. military to help soldiers determine locations. But in 2000, the U.S. government made the system widely available to the public.

Entrepreneurs pounced. Some created GPS devices to help keep wilderness hikers from getting lost. Companies such as TomTom put this technology in cars, along with software to calculate the best route for drivers to follow. As GPS devices became smaller, they went into cell phones and cameras, allowing photographers to **geotag** photographs. Other companies used it to track the location of delivery vehicles.

GPS systems can even warn drivers about traffic delays.

The New Space Age

Even though businesses compete with each other, entrepreneurs often share their ideas and research with one another. Established in 2016, the New Space Age Conference is an annual gathering at which space entrepreneurs present some of their products and talk about the latest developments in technology. By sharing stories and ideas, entrepreneurs work together to push space innovation forward.

Presenters have included Dr. Natalya Bailey of Accion Systems; Ellen Chang, a founder at LightSpeed Innovations; and Dr. Erika Wagner of Blue Origin. Students at MIT also presented their research on some of the latest technologies.

Sharing satellite data will help us learn more about our planet and its processes.

SPACE DATA
START-UP STAR:
DAN BERKENSTOCK

Dan Berkenstock was a 27-year-old Ph.D. student at Stanford University when Google announced the Lunar X Prize. The competition, launched in 2007, offered a $20 million prize. It was to be awarded to any privately funded team that could land a rover on the Moon, take pictures, and send them back to Earth. Berkenstock tried to raise money to develop a rover to enter in the competition. But his investors pulled out during the **financial crisis** in 2008. Though he did not succeed, he learned how to work with other people toward a big goal, and he was hooked on space.

Berkenstock created Skybox satellites. These powerful satellites can take pictures from space. The photos are detailed enough to see cars and shipping containers on Earth!

BUILDING THE TEAM

Berkenstock teamed up with John Fenwick and Julian Mann, fellow Stanford students in their 20s, to found Skybox Imaging. They had partnered with him on the Lunar X Prize attempt. Fenwick was with the U.S. Air Force, and Mann had founded his own space-related company Astronautical Development. They were joined by another former Stanford student, Ching-Yu Hu. She had analyzed data for banking company J.P. Morgan, so she knew how to raise cash for Berkenstock, Fenwick, and Mann's business plan.

Skybox Imaging's business plan was to build and send small, cheap satellites into orbit to collect data and send it back to Earth. The lightweight satellites could be sent up on smaller rockets, further reducing costs. Despite this simple plan, Skybox had trouble finding investors. People were not sure if the plan would work. However, Skybox raised enough money to launch its first satellite, SkySat-1, on November 2013. It began transmitting data and sending pictures a few days later.

Skybox's offices are located in Mountain View, California.

SPECIALIZED DATA

Skybox promised to collect data that was not picked up by the other satellites. Instead of widespread weather patterns, Skybox satellites could look at how well crops are growing on individual farms. Skybox satellites could be used to monitor a network of drones delivering packages down on the ground. Larger satellites collected more generalized data, but Skybox promised that its cheaper, lighter satellites could collect images of specific places, objects, and events.

GOOGLE MAKES AN OFFER

In June 2014, Google announced it was buying Berkenstock's company for $500 million—a much bigger prize from Google than Berkenstock competed for back in 2007. Google took on Skybox's satellites as a way to expand its Internet services, particularly Google Earth and Google Maps.

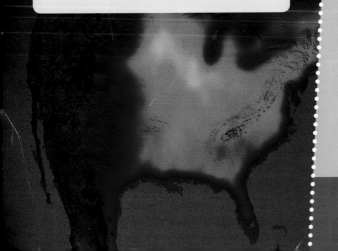

Satellites can see things that are invisible to us on the ground. This image shows the faint glow of corn crops in the eastern United States.

MINES IN SPACE

We rely on natural resources on Earth every day. They provide everything from the energy used to power homes and vehicles to the water we drink. We mine materials, such as metals, from Earth's crust to use in manufacturing or to wear as jewelry. But the natural resources on Earth are limited. Some cannot be replaced. This means that before too long, we could run out of the resources we rely on—unless we can get them from space.

ROBOT MINERS

It takes a lot of energy to send a machine into space. It takes even more to send a person, and supply them with food, water, and oxygen. So when it comes to mining asteroids, it may be simpler to send robots. Or is it? Mining is hard enough for people. How do we teach robots what minerals to look for and how to find them? How do we design them with the right tools and equipment to get the job done?

Even if we send robots to mine asteroids, it is still expensive to send machines so far into space. Then there is the question of getting all of the material they mine back to Earth. If something goes wrong, it would be almost impossible to send someone to fix the problem.

This artist's concept shows a NASA plan to capture a small asteroid for study.

LIQUID GOLD

But maybe people would not be as far away as we think. Asteroids and the other planets might provide valuable **raw materials**. These materials would be useful for building colonies on other worlds. These colonies might be set up on comets and asteroids, acting as refueling stations for passing ships. A colony on the Moon might make money as a launch pad. It takes less energy to launch a rocket from the Moon than from Earth. Space start-ups that set up refueling stations and launch pads could be a key part of expanding humanity out into space.

Perhaps one day the Moon might be a launch pad for space travel!

Mining the Moon

American company Moon Express was founded in 2010 by Naveen Jain. Its goal is to mine the Moon, which could be easier than mining asteroids. The Moon is closer to Earth than most asteroids. Also, millions of meteors have struck the Moon, which has showered minerals and metals all over the surface. This means they will not have to dig deep to make money. Moon Express is working on robotic ships that will map and test the Moon's surface. They will eventually bring back material.

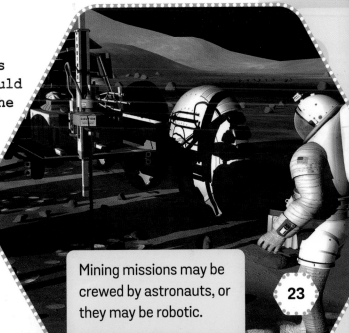

Mining missions may be crewed by astronauts, or they may be robotic.

START-UP STAR:
CHRIS LEWICKI

Chris Lewicki studied aerospace engineering at the University of Arizona and went on to work for NASA. He rose to the level of flight director for the Mars Exploration Rover (MER) missions of Spirit and Opportunity. He was the surface mission manager for the Phoenix lander. He even had an asteroid named in his honor: 13609 Lewicki.

A NEW IDEA

Lewicki decided to leave NASA to start up a company called Planetary Resources in 2009 with Eric Anderson and Peter Diamandis. The company wants to **harvest** natural resources from asteroids, such as minerals and water. However, they do not plan to bring them back to Earth. They feel that the real value of space

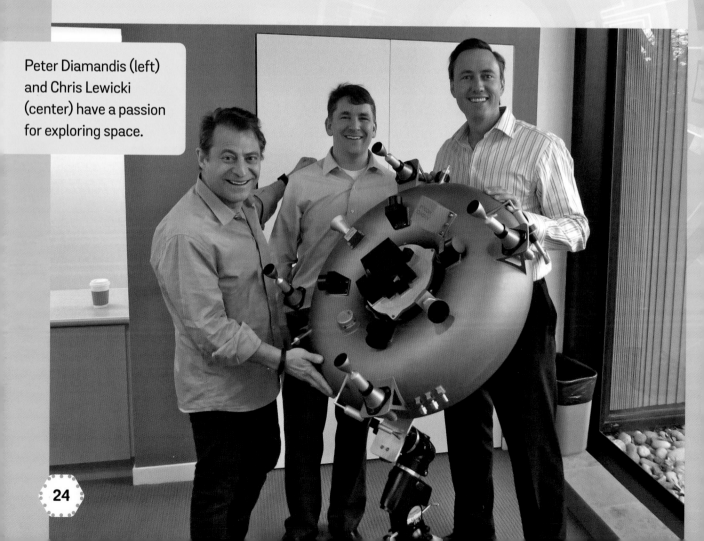

Peter Diamandis (left) and Chris Lewicki (center) have a passion for exploring space.

24

It may be possible for humans to mine asteroids. However, the risks may make sending robots a safer option.

resources is their continued use in space. For example, certain types of asteroids are made of up to 20 percent water. Water harvested from asteroids could be used on other planets for drinking and for growing plants. It could even be split into oxygen to use for breathing and hydrogen for rocket fuel. Harvesting the water from asteroids means that it would not need to be transported from Earth. That would save money and greatly reduce the load a rocket must carry.

SMALL STEPS

Lewicki knew his idea was ambitious. It had cost NASA $1 billion to build and operate Spirit and Opportunity. Even sending unmanned probes into space to land on another planet or asteroid is expensive. So, Planetary Resources

started out by building space telescopes to survey near–Earth asteroids. They used lasers that allowed the telescopes to communicate with control centers on Earth. The company hopes to use the information they gather to later harvest asteroid resources.

BLASTING INTO SPACE

Planetary Resources built its first satellite, the Arkyd–3. It was launched on a SpaceX rocket to the International Space Station on April 14, 2015. The satellite began flight testing the following July, and the spacecraft test was successful. Planetary Resources is currently working on a second satellite—the larger Arkyd–6. It is building up to its long-term goal of harvesting resources from asteroids.

THE NEW SPACE RACE

Science and space have gone together throughout history. Sir Isaac Newton used mathematics to predict the orbits of planets. Since then, our understanding of the universe has increased as our abilities in science, technology, engineering, and mathematics have increased. The United States and the Soviet Union raced into space. The United States got there thanks to the mathematical brilliance of people such as Mary Jackson and Katherine Johnson, and the coding work of Margaret Hamilton.

SPACE EXPLORERS

For years, space exploration was only done by governments with the time and money to overcome its challenges. But as technology improved, start-up stars began creating businesses related to space technology and exploration. They made their own satellites to send messages around the world. They used space to gather data from places humans could not go before. Space entrepreneurs changed our understanding of the world, and brought us all in closer contact with each other.

The entrepreneurs in today's space race are involved because of the profit they see in space. However, they also hope to benefit the whole human race. They have seen the new products and services the space race has

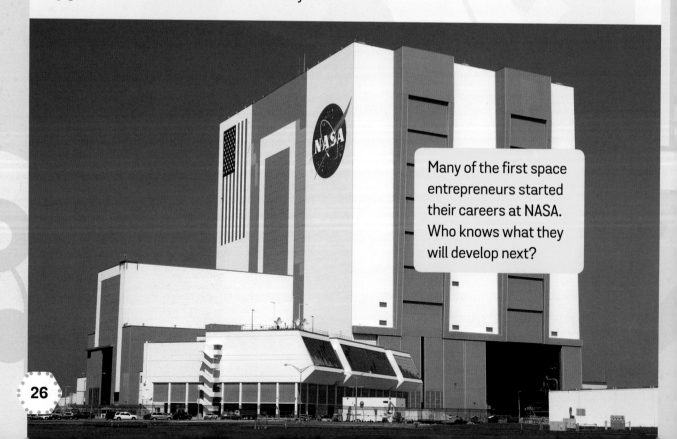

Many of the first space entrepreneurs started their careers at NASA. Who knows what they will develop next?

given us. They are excited about what the future holds, and they want everyone else to be excited, too. For many space entrepreneurs, getting people excited about new space exploration could mean sending people to live on Mars or other planets. This would ensure that the human race could live on if something happens to Earth.

START-UPS ARE THE FUTURE

Throughout history, young students have changed our understanding of space. It has been young entrepreneurs who have invented technologies that have taken us into space. From Sir Isaac Newton to Elon Musk, these people have shown that, in the future, young entrepreneurs will find the next **breakthroughs** and take the next steps. Perhaps you might one day follow in their footsteps. Maybe your journey could even take you to Mars—or beyond!

Maybe these young scientists will be the next space entrepreneurs!

Why not use your science and technology skills to build an amazing career in space science?

27

YOUR START-UP STORY

As our understanding of science and mathematics has improved, so too has our understanding of space. We have learned to predict the movement of planets and plan the flight of rockets. We have sent satellites into orbit, landed people on the Moon, and sent probes to Mars and beyond. Through it all, our dreams for space have grown. We have imagined building colonies on other planets. Space is widely viewed as a new frontier, with tremendous challenges, but with opportunities to improve lives.

TAKE THE START-UP CHALLENGE!

Space is a hard place to get to and work in. The distances are huge. The environment cannot support life. A lot of energy is required to get out of Earth's orbit. It takes a lot of hard work and math to make spaceships land in certain places, so they can be reused. All of this makes going to space very expensive, but scientists and entrepreneurs are working to change that.

All entrepreneurs begin with an idea. To take it to the market, they research their idea, and look at ways it solves a problem or meets a need. Successful entrepreneurs choose fields they like working in, or activities they like doing. Think about where you can research more about the fields or activities you are interested in. Figure out ways you can use your research to help people. Think of ways you might convince other people to support your ideas. The activity on the next page is a way to kick off your entrepreneurial career.

How will you launch your career as a space entrepreneur?

START-UP CHALLENGE
COULD YOU COLONIZE MARS?

Entrepreneurs such as Elon Musk believe that the human race needs to set up a colony on Mars. Technology could one day make it possible for humans to live there. That would mean that if anything happened to Earth, the human race could survive—on Mars.

Here are some questions asked by scientists hoping to colonize Mars. Think back to some of the ideas and innovations you read about in this book. Can you use your science and technology skills to find possible solutions?

- How would you get to Mars?
- What would you have to bring with you?
- How could you send the supplies you need?
- How could you make things that you need while on Mars?
- A goal is for an eventual Mars colony to be self-sufficient. This means that it can support itself. What would it take for a colony to be self-sufficient on Mars?

Science centers are a fun way to learn more about science and technology.

Write down your questions, and **brainstorm** some possible answers. Look things up online and at your local library. Explore, and see what ideas come to you. Perhaps you can find a need that you could fulfill with a brilliant new entrepreneurial idea!

You are never too young to start getting interested in space and technology!

GLOSSARY

aerospace Industry and technology that deals with planes and space flight

asteroids Small rocky objects that orbit the Sun; asteroids are smaller than planets

bankrupt Having a lot of debt and no money to pay that debt

brainstorm A way a team solves problems by sharing a lot of ideas all at once and deciding which ones are the best to follow

breakthroughs Sudden and important discoveries

budget The amount of money someone is allowed to spend over a given time

capsule A small spacecraft, or the part of a larger spacecraft that contains the instruments and crew

CEO (short for **Chief Executive Officer**) A person who is in charge of a company

colony Group of people who have left their homeland to set up new settlements in a new land

drone ship A driverless ship that is controlled remotely

entrepreneurs People who create a business, and take on most of the risk to operate it

environment The conditions around something, such as temperature, humidity, and quality of air

extraterrestrial Not from Earth

fertilizer A substance, such as manure, that is full of nutrients that help plants grow

financial crisis A period around 2008 when banks around the world collapsed and a lot of people lost a lot of money

first stage booster rocket The part of a rocket that provides the fuel for the takeoff thrust

geosynchronous orbit An orbit around Earth that matches Earth's rotation on its axis

geotag An electronic tag assigned to a digital photograph or piece of data to show its location on Earth

global positioning system (GPS) The system that uses satellites to detect where things are on Earth

global warming Heating of Earth's atmosphere caused by increased levels of carbon dioxide and other pollutants

goods Products; something made to be sold

harvest Gather something up to take it away

innovative Describing something that no one else has done before

International Space Station (ISS) A base that orbits Earth and holds a crew of up to six astronauts

interpret Explain, or figure out, the meaning of something

investors People who give you money to start a business, in return for owning a share of that business

ions Atoms with more or fewer than the normal number of electrons, giving them an electrical charge

meteorologists Scientists who study Earth's atmosphere and its weather

microgravity When gravity is very weak, such as on an orbiting space station

minerals Inorganic materials, such as metal or stone

oasis An area in a desert where water is found and plants can be grown

orbit To move around something, like a moon around a planet

overpopulation Having too many people for the amount of space and resources available in the area

parabolas Symmetrical curves or paths

radar A way of measuring or detecting something by sending out electromagnetic waves that bounce off the object back to the source

raw materials Unprocessed natural materials, such as minerals, metals, or wood, that are used to make other things

resources The money, supplies, people, and energy required to make things happen

satellite Any object that orbits another object; satellites can be natural or made by people

services Types of help or work that someone does for someone else

slide rules Rulers with a sliding piece for making mathematical calculations

Soviet Union A large country in northern Asia and eastern Europe that existed between 1917 and 1991, which included today's Russia and 14 other republics

triangulation Figuring out where something is by measuring the distance to it from two other known points

LEARNING MORE

BOOKS

Aldrin, Buzz, and Marianne J. Dyson. *Welcome to Mars: Making a Home on the Red Planet*. National Geographic, 2015.

Baker, David, and Heather Kissock. *Satellites* (Exploring Space). Weigl, 2017.

Buckley Jr, James. *Space Exploration* (The Solar System). Mason Crest, 2017.

Cameron, Schyrlet, and Carolyn Craig. *STEM Labs for Middle Grades: 50+ Integrated Labs*. Mark Twain Media, 2016.

Dyson, Marianne J. *A Passion for Space: Adventures of a Pioneering Female NASA Flight Controller*. Springer Praxis Books, 2016.

Nagelhout, Ryan. *Elon Musk: Space Entrepreneur* (People in the News). Lucent Press, 2017.

WEBSITES

BizKids
bizkids.com
A website teaching kids how to watch their money and handle business. Features videos, lesson plans, games, and a blog.

Engineer Girl
www.engineergirl.org
A site encouraging girls and young women to join the exciting field of engineering, including interviews, competitions, and career advice.

Astronomy for Kids
www.astronomy.com/observing/astro-for-kids
A resource for kids and teens to learn about outer space, other worlds, and our own place in the universe.

NASA
nasa.gov
The official site for NASA. Learn about its programs and discoveries. Includes sections for all ages.

INDEX

ABOUT THE AUTHOR

James Bow is the author of more than 40 educational books for children and young adults. He is also a novelist and a columnist, and holds a degree in Urban and Regional Planning.